When we are asked,
"Where is Your God?"
We know
that we know
what we know
and can respond
in great confidence.

Copyright © 2023 by Stephanie D. Moore

Published by
Moore Marketing and Communications, LLC

Oklahoma City, OK
StephanieDMoore.com
MooretoRead.com

In accordance with the U.S. Copyright Act of 1976, scanning, uploading, or electronic sharing of any part of this book, audio, written, or e-published is strictly prohibited and unlawful. No part of this book may be reproduced in any form by any means, including photocopying, electronic, mechanical, recording, or by any information storage and retrieval systems without permission in writing by the copyright owner.

Bulk copies or group sales of this book are available by contacting Stephanie D. Moore at moore@stephaniedmoore.com or (405) 306-9833.

Moore, Stephanie D.
Where Is YOUR God?
A 31-Day Devotional

Edited by Debra M. Smith

First Edition Printed May 2023
Printed in the USA.

Cover Design and Layout Design by
Moore Marketing and Communications, LLC.
All Rights Reserved.

Cover Photo used in design retrieved at pexels.com,
taken by RDNE Stock Project..

ISBN: 978-1-955544-41-2

Why do the nations say, "Where is their God?"
Psalm 115:2

Where is
YOUR God?

In Loving Memory

Michael & Brenda Bradley

The Lord is my strength and my shield;
my heart trusts in him, and he helps me.
My heart leaps for joy,
and with my song I praise him.
Psalm 28:7

Whatever Pleases Him

Why do the nations say, "Where is their God?"

Psalm 115:2

Why would someone care where your God is? Perhaps it is because they can sense his presence when you enter a room or maybe they experience his love when you are attentive to their needs. Maybe it is because you are as bold as a lion and as harmless as a dove. It could be that they are a witness to your struggle, but you refuse to lose faith. Only God knows why one's curiosity would peak so greatly as to question the location of your God.

A relationship with God is required for those who wish to understand his greatness. God is omnipotent, omniscient, omnibenevolent, and omnipresent. Anything he desires is his. All that we see, know and experience has either been created by him or allowed to exist by his authority. God is not an instrument that can be utilized to gain power, money, authority, or fame. He doesn't sit as a statue - motionless and unable to speak.

He is. He was. He will be.

Those who trust God are protected and blessed. His name is glorified throughout the earth. His presence is a healing balm. His instructions are a rushing water making crooked places straight.

In response to his faithfulness and enduring love, we give him honor and seek him first. We worship him so that we may yet understand his will. We trust him so that we may have his Holy Spirit to guide us.

Jesus died so that we may live. When he arose, he did so with all power in his hand. Jesus is the Living Word of God, he has imparted us with his Holy Spirit, and we all reside in the body of Christ.

The same God that rescued us from a life of sin, cherished David as a man after his own heart and led him to become king. The same God who kept us safe from the harm of our enemies befriended Abraham and counted his faith as righteousness. The same God who provided for our families, making a way out of no way, fed his prophet Elijah by a brook during a drought. The same God who led us into our promised land, led the Israelites from the captivity of Pharaoh in Egypt.

When we are asked, where is our God? We know that we know what we know and can respond in great confidence. "Our God is in heaven, and he does whatever pleases him."

Prayer

Most Gracious and Heavenly Father,

You are our shepherd, we lack nothing. You make us lie down in green pastures, you lead us beside quiet waters, you refresh our souls. You guide us along the right paths for your name's sake. Even though we walk through the darkest valley, we will fear no evil, for you are with us; your rod and your staff, they comfort us. You prepare a table before us in the presence of our enemies. You anoint our heads with oil; our cup overflows. Surely your goodness and love will follow us all the days of our lives, and we will dwell in the house of the Lord forever. [(1)]

In Jesus' Name,
Amen

The Lord is Our Refuge

The field commander said to them, "Tell Hezekiah: "This is what the great king, the king of Assyria, says: On what are you basing this confidence of yours? You say you have the counsel and the might for war—but you speak only empty words. On whom are you depending, that you rebel against me?"

2 Kings 18:19-20

King Sennacherib had already seized the land of Israel and exiled their people to Assyria when he elected to attack Jerusalem. However, the King of Israel, Hoshea, did evil in the sight of God and led his people astray, subjecting them to attack. King Hezekiah, a faithful servant of God and good leader, also rebelled against King Sennacherib and refused to bow down to his threats. But he was a good king and trusted the Lord.

When God allows you to succeed in the face of your enemies or allows you to display your confidence in His ability to see you through, your enemies will not only attack you - but they will attack your God. They will attempt to destroy your character. They will attempt to destroy your faith. They will attempt to destroy the relationship you have with those who protect you and those you protect. They will do these things in the sight of an audience to bolster their disrespect and to try and belittle your confidence. The evidence of their attempt to dissuade, seduce and enchant will be the lies they spew without waver.

This is a mind game. When those who are closest to us enact weapons of war, it is our responsibility to allow God to fight the battle. Move out of his way. Our enemies think that their success is going to defeat the sovereignty of God in their situation, but God is going to show them his power.

When we are asked, where is our God? We know that we know what we know and can respond in great confidence. We will say of the Lord, "He is our refuge and our fortress, our God, in whom we trust." (2)

Prayer

Most Gracious and Heavenly Father,

If we say, "The Lord is our refuge," and we make the Most High our dwelling, no harm will overtake us, no disaster will come near our tent. For he will command his angels concerning us to guard us in all of our ways; they will lift us up in their hands, so that we will not strike our foot against a stone. We will tread on the lion and the cobra; we will trample the great lion and the serpent. "Because they love me," says the Lord, "I will rescue them; I will protect them, for they acknowledge my name. They will call on me, and I will answer them; I will be with them in trouble, I will deliver them and honor them. With long life I will satisfy them and show them my salvation." (3)

In Jesus' Name,
Amen

Prepared for Opportunity

David asked the men standing near him, "What will be done for the man who kills this Philistine and removes this disgrace from Israel? Who is this uncircumcised Philistine that he should defy the armies of the living God?"

1 Samuel 17:26

Our personal responsibilities will always prepare us for our next opportunity. As we pursue those opportunities, we must respect what is required for our current state. Likewise, as we begin to rise in our expectations and desires, we will be taunted, attacked, and belittled.

David was a young and responsible shepherd. One day as the Israelites and the Philistines were in battle formation (an event that had taken place day in and day out for more than 40 days), David's father sent him to the battle with food for his brothers, to find out what was happening, and to encourage his siblings.

David did as he was asked. But before he left, he made sure that another shepherd was tending his sheep.

David also made sure that all his equipment was stored and being cared for. Then he went to the battle to do what his father instructed him to do.

When David arrived, he found an army of men who were afraid of one specific man in the Philistine army - Goliath. Goliath was large and menacing. He verbally attacked the Israelites at every opportunity. David looked at the man as no more of a threat than one of the beasts of the fields that threatened his sheep on a daily basis. He knew that if he could survive those animals and protect his sheep, he could defeat Goliath and protect the Israelites.

David asked what the man who would be able to defeat Goliath would gain. While he inquired, his brothers overheard him and taunted him. But David ignored their taunts and instead focused on upleveling his position by defeating an enemy of God's army.

David rose to the challenge despite the king himself questioning his ability. When the king tried to give David the tools he imagined he would need to succeed, David denied them knowing exactly what he needed to do in order to defeat Goliath. He also knew that this was not a battle he would even have to fight, but that by simply giving the battle to God, victory already belonged to him.

David not only defeated Goliath, but he did so on his first attempt. By honoring his responsibilities, he was prepared for a battle no other soldier was fit or able to fight. In his obedience, David was in the right place at the right time. By having faith in God, he was able to win a battle he should not have been able to fight and gain the favor of the king. The taunts and doubt those around him had before the battle began disappeared and was replaced with praise, disbelief, and honor. No one knew that David had the ability to fight such a battle, but David had been prepared by God because he was faithful to do what God instructed when no one was looking.

When we are asked, where is our God? We know that we know what we know and can respond in great confidence. We will say of the Lord with boldness before our enemies, "You come against me with sword and spear and javelin, but I come against you in the name of the Lord Almighty, the God of the armies of Israel, whom you have defied. This day the Lord will deliver you into my hands, and I'll strike you down and cut off your head. This very day I will give the carcasses of the Philistine army to the birds and the wild animals, and the whole world will know that there is a God in Israel. All those gathered here will know that it is not by sword or spear that the Lord saves; for the battle is the Lord's, and he will give all of you into our hands." (4)

Prayer

Most Gracious and Heavenly Father,

Rescue us from our enemies, Lord, for we hide ourselves in you. Teach us to do your will, for you are our God; may your good Spirit lead us on level ground. For your name's sake, Lord, preserve our lives; in your righteousness, bring us out of trouble. In your unfailing love, silence our enemies; destroy all of our foes, for we are your servants. (5)

In Jesus' Name,
Amen

Trouble Behind Me. . . Joy Before Me

Pharaoh said, "Who is the Lord, that I should obey him and let Israel go? I do not know the Lord and I will not let Israel go."

Exodus 5:2

When people question our worship, look past our confession, and see our poor circumstance and count it as evidence, they demand the presence of God to be known. God will not be mocked.

Pharaoh was an Egyptian ruler who managed his kingdom with the counsel of magicians. When the Israelites grew in number in Egypt after the death of Joseph, the Egyptian leaders who did not know Joseph did not respect the lineage of the Israelites and decided to make them their slaves. God heard the cries of the Israelites because of the hard burdens the Egyptians had placed on them and sent Moses to rescue them.

God sent Moses, who felt he was the least likely person to speak publicly, to demand that Pharoah allow the Israelites to worship him in the desert. Despite plea after plea for Pharaoh to let them go and worship God, he refused to let them go. Instead, Pharaoh took away the necessary tools for the Israelites to work and doubled their workload causing them great anguish and confusion. But God promised to deliver the Israelites.

In response, God made certain that Pharaoh and all the Egyptians knew that God was sovereign, and it was he who had the ultimate authority. God spoke through Moses and gave him and Aaron the ability to perform miracles and wonders never seen before the leadership of Egypt. In Pharaoh's stubbornness he forced God to issue the plagues of blood, frogs, gnats, flies, the plague on the livestock, the plagues of boils, hail, locusts, and the plague of darkness that could be felt upon the people of Egypt. Then he issued the plague of the first-born, which killed every first born son of the Egyptians and their livestock because Pharaoh refused to allow God's first-born son, Israel to worship him.

After the ultimate ruin of Egypt and the sorrow of losing his first born son, Pharaoh finally relented in allowing the Israelites to go and worship God. But no sooner had they left than his anger arose, and he pursued them again. But God was encamped around the Israelites in protection and when Pharaoh and his army pursued them, they fell privy to their own defeat, dying beneath the crushing waves of the Red Sea.

When we are asked, where is our God? We know that we know what we know and can respond in great confidence. We will say of the Lord, "Come and see what God has done, his awesome deeds for mankind! He turned the sea into dry land, they passed through the waters on foot—come, let us rejoice in him. He rules forever by his power, his eyes watch the nations—let not the rebellious rise up against him." [(6)]

Prayer

Most Gracious and Heavenly Father,

Praise our God, all peoples, let the sound of his praise be heard; he has preserved our lives and kept our feet from slipping. For you, God, tested us; you refined us like silver. You brought us into prison and laid burdens on our backs. You let people ride over our heads; we went through fire and water, but you brought us to a place of abundance. We will come to your temple with burnt offerings and fulfill our vows to you—vows our lips promised and our mouths spoke when we were in trouble. We will sacrifice fat animals to you and an offering of rams; we will offer bulls and goats. Come and hear, all you who fear God; let us tell you what he has done for us. We cried out to him with our mouths; his praise was on our tongues. If we had cherished sin in our hearts, the Lord would not have listened; but God has surely listened and has heard our prayers. Praise be to God, who has not rejected our prayers or withheld his love from us! [(7)]

In Jesus' Name,
Amen

Faith in Action

Jesus was in the stern, sleeping on a cushion. The disciples woke him and said to him, "Teacher, don't you care if we drown?"

Mark 4:38

Every principle that God teaches in the Bible is at first explained and later exemplified through experiential stories therefore producing wisdom through the application of knowledge.

When Jesus spoke to the crowd explaining how the kingdom of God represented seeds planted in different conditions which may or may not lead to a harvest, he was teaching the disciples about faith. Those who embraced faith could reap an exponential harvest of believers through actions empowered by the Holy Spirit.

Jesus was preparing his disciples to continue the work of spreading the gospel after he left the earth. The people needed to see miracles and wonders to believe but that required the disciples to perform them in faith.

The disciples needed to experience situations that

could only be resolved through faith in Christ and his ability to perform, even when he wasn't present.

Jesus sent them out in pairs to preach, he fed the 5,000 with less than enough, and he placed them in a storm as he slept in the bottom of the boat. At each opportunity, Jesus wanted the disciples to learn to exercise their faith to solve complex issues.

His teaching worked and the seeds of the gospel were watered through miracles performed through faith. Paul and Silas praised God to be released from prison. Peter preached and converted 3,000 souls to Christ. Peter and John healed a man that laid by a gate called Beautiful. Paul got bitten by a poisonous snake and was unharmed. Peter was freed by an angel as the church prayed for his release.

When we are asked, where is our God? We know that we know what we know and can respond in great confidence. We will say to those who question the Lord, "In the beginning was the Word, and the Word was with God, and the Word was God. He was with God in the beginning. Through him all things were made; without him nothing was made that has been made. In him was life, and that life was the light of all mankind. The light shines in the darkness, and the darkness has not overcome it." [8]

Prayer

Most Gracious and Heavenly Father,

By faith we understand that the universe was formed at God's command, so that what is seen was not made out of what was visible. By faith Abel brought God a better offering than Cain did. By faith he was commended as righteous, when God spoke well of his offerings. And by faith Abel still speaks, even though he is dead. By faith Enoch was taken from this life, so that he did not experience death: "He could not be found, because God had taken him away." For before he was taken, he was commended as one who pleased God. And without faith it is impossible to please God, because anyone who comes to him must believe that he exists and that he rewards those who earnestly seek him. (9)

In Jesus' Name,
Amen

Build in the Face of Opposition

Hear us, our God, for we are despised. Turn their insults back on their own heads. Give them over as plunder in a land of captivity. Do not cover up their guilt or blot out their sins from your sight, for they have thrown insults in the face of the builders.

Nehemiah 4:4-5

We were each created for a unique purpose. If we are blessed enough to discover that purpose and work toward the goals that God places before us, we must know we will face opposition.

Satan desires to kill, steal, and destroy whatever and whoever God has chosen to bless. But God came that we might have a good life filled with his peace, restoration, and blessings.

When the Israelites returned to Jerusalem to rebuild the city after their season of captivity, they were met with local people who did not want to see them restored. In fact, the local men went out of their way to prevent them from succeeding. So much so, that the families who worked diligently were forced to pray and have guards protecting them day and night to ensure the work was finished.

Despite being protected, the local men continued to plot to end the rebuilding of the city gates. No matter what the Israelites were doing, or where they were, the local men tried to attack them. The Israelites remained focused and devised a way to work together to protect themselves. But the people were poor, in debt and some had children who were forced into slavery. The irony is that those who were supposed to be their neighbors (as some were Jews returning from exile and others were in the land prior to them) were the ones overcharging them and taking advantage of them. Nehemiah put a stop to that immediately and soon became governor. During his reign, rather than take from the people he made sure the city was rebuilt and the people were cared for.

When we are asked, where is our God? We know that we know what we know and can respond in great confidence. We will say, "We will not be afraid of them. We remember the Lord, who is great and awesome, and will fight for our families, our sons and our daughters, our wives and our homes." [10]

Prayer

Most Gracious and Heavenly Father,

Keep us safe, our God, for in you we take refuge. We say to the Lord, "You are our Lord; apart from you we have no good thing." We say of the holy people who are in the land, "They are the noble ones in whom is all our delight." Those who run after other gods will suffer more and more. We will not pour out libations of blood to such gods or take up their names on our lips. Lord, you alone are our portion and our cup; you make our lot secure. The boundary lines have fallen for us in pleasant places; surely we have a delightful inheritance. We will praise the Lord, who counsels us; even at night our heart instructs us. We keep our eyes always on the Lord. With him at our right hand, we will not be shaken. Therefore our heart is glad and our tongue rejoices; our body also will rest secure, because you will not abandon us to the realm of the dead, nor will you let our faithful one see decay. You make known to us the path of life; you will fill us with joy in your presence, with eternal pleasures at your right hand. [(11)]

In Jesus' Name,
Amen

Every Plot of the Enemy is Destroyed

When Haman saw that Mordecai would not kneel down or pay him honor, he was enraged. Yet having learned who Mordecai's people were, he scorned the idea of killing only Mordecai. Instead Haman looked for a way to destroy all Mordecai's people, the Jews, throughout the whole kingdom of Xerxes.

Esther 3:5-6

When we refuse to place satanic power or those who wield it above our beliefs and worship of God, our destruction becomes a goal of the enemy. First, he will try to destroy our honor. When that is unable to be accomplished, he will try to destroy us and everything we have. But God bears witness to every plot of the enemy and will destroy every weapon forged against us.

Mordecai was a man of God, and he raised a young woman of God. When it was time for the King Xerxes to find a new queen, he chose Esther, Mordecai's niece. Mordecai worked for the king at the king's gate. One day, he overheard a plot to kill the king and sent word to Queen Esther and the plot was thwarted. Afterward, a man named Haman was promoted to second in command in the kingdom.

When Haman saw Mordecai at the gate, he demanded that Mordecai show him honor by bowing down to him (as all the other guards did), but Mordecai refused. When Haman did some research, he discovered that it was because of Mordecai's Jewish background that he refused to honor him. So he decided to not only get rid of Mordecai, but everyone that practiced his faith and belonged to his heritage. Haman did not know the queen was a part of their family. Haman convinced the king to sign a decree that would allow him to destroy, annihilate and kill every Jew in their entire country.

When Mordecai found out he was depressed and sent word to Queen Esther demanding she do something to save their people. Esther and all the Jews fasted for three days, after which, Esther risked her life to approach the king. She invited him and Haman to dinner. When they came to dinner the king asked her what she wanted as he was willing to give her up to half of the kingdom if she only requested it. She asked the two men to return and have dinner with her again the next night.

Haman couldn't enjoy his fellowship with the king and queen because of his hatred of Mordecai. He would not be happy until the man was dead. Haman's wife suggested he build a pole to kill Mordecai publicly. Haman did it. The next day, he awoke determined to kill Mordecai but was instead met with a request from the king to honor Mordecai. Haman was confused and disgruntled as it was his personal responsibility to see that Mordecai was esteemed with honor.

Later that evening when he went to dinner with the king and queen, the king again asked Esther what she desired. She then revealed that she needed the king to rid her of her enemy, someone who plotted to kill her and all her people, Haman. The king was outraged. The servants revealed that Haman had even built a way to kill Mordecai and that it was prepared. The king instructed them to kill Haman on the 75-foot pole instead of killing Mordecai.

The edict that was written was immediately reversed. All that belonged to Haman was given to Esther. Mordecai was promoted. All the enemies of the Jews were destroyed.

When we are asked, where is our God? We know that we know what we know and can respond in great confidence. We will say of the Lord, "For our name's sake, the Lord will preserve our lives; in his righteousness, he will bring us out of trouble. In his unfailing love, he will silence our enemies; and destroy all our foes, for we are his servants. [12] No weapon formed against us shall be able to prosper and every tongue that rises against us shall be condemned for this is the heritage of the saints of the Lord. [13]"

Prayer

Most Gracious and Heavenly Father,

Our God, whom we praise, do not remain silent, for people who are wicked and deceitful have opened their mouths against us; they have spoken against us with lying tongues. With words of hatred, they surround us; they attack us without cause. In return for our friendship, they accuse us, but we are a people of prayer. They repay us evil for good, and hatred for our friendship. Appoint someone evil to oppose our enemy; let an accuser stand at his right hand. When he is tried, let him be found guilty, and may his prayers condemn him. May his days be few; may another take his place of leadership. May his children be fatherless and his wife a widow. May his children be wandering beggars; may they be driven from their ruined homes. May a creditor seize all he has; may strangers plunder the fruits of his labor. May no one extend kindness to him or take pity on his fatherless children. May his descendants be cut off, their names blotted out from the next generation. May the iniquity of his fathers be remembered before the Lord; may the sin of his mother never be blotted out. May their sins always remain before the Lord, that he may blot out their name from the earth. For he never thought of doing a kindness, but hounded to death the poor and the needy and the brokenhearted. He loved to pronounce a curse—may it come back on him. He found no pleasure in blessing—may it be far from him. He wore cursing as his garment; it entered into his body like water, into his bones like oil. May it be like a cloak wrapped about him, like a belt tied forever around him. May this be the Lord's payment to my accusers, to those who speak evil of us. But you, Sovereign Lord, help us for your name's sake; out of the goodness of your love, deliver us. For we are poor and needy, and our hearts are wounded within us. We fade away like an evening shadow; we are shaken off like a locust. Our knees give way from fasting; our body is thin and gaunt. We are an object of scorn to our accusers; when they see us, they shake their heads. Help us, Lord our God; save us according to your unfailing love. Let them know that it is your hand, that you, Lord, have done it. While they curse, may you bless; may those who attack me be put to shame, but may your servant rejoice. May our accusers be clothed with disgrace and wrapped in shame as in a cloak. With our mouths we will greatly extol the Lord; in the great throng of worshipers we will praise him. For he stands at the right hand of the needy, to save their lives from those who would condemn them.[14]

In Jesus' Name,
Amen

Safe in His Arms

Stay with me; don't be afraid. The man who wants to kill you is trying to kill me too. You will be safe with me.

I Samuel 22:23

I grew up hearing the phrase, "The enemy of my enemy is my friend."

But the way God expresses it in scripture is, "See, I am sending an angel ahead of you to guard you along the way and to bring you to the place I have prepared. Pay attention to him and listen to what he says. Do not rebel against him; he will not forgive your rebellion, since my Name is in him. If you listen carefully to what he says and do all that I say, I will be an enemy to your enemies and will oppose those who oppose you. My angel will go ahead of you and bring you into the land of the Amorites, Hittites, Perizzites, Canaanites, Hivites and Jebusites, and I will wipe them out."

When we face undeniable opposition, it is good to have someone on our side that will fight for us, protect us, guide us, hide us, or simply warn us of what is coming.

In the Bible, David served King Saul in many ways. He always did so with a smile on his face and good intentions in his heart. But Saul grew jealous of David and wanted him dead. Saul's ill intentions for David grew with such passion that Saul's own son wanted to protect David from his father. David ran away. During his escape, he went to visit a priest, Ahimelek, that prayed for him often. While there, a loyal and evil servant of Saul saw David and told Saul where he could be found.

When the priest, Ahimelek, refused to tell Saul the direction David had gone, Saul ordered for the priest and all 85 of the priests living in that community to be killed because they too refused to tell Saul where David had fled. But Saul's soldiers refused to touch the men of God. So, the evil servant who reported David's whereabouts killed all 85 of them instead. When the son of the high priest escaped, he ran straight to David to report what had transpired.

David, a mighty and great warrior of God, promised the young man that he would protect him.

David had a unique and special purpose on his life. He would eventually take hold of Jerusalem, naming it the City of God. The lineage of Jesus Christ would fall within his bloodline. The enemy of David was essentially the enemy of God. The priests risked their lives to save David because of his anointing.

Soon after, God gave David the opportunity to avenge the death of the priests and to kill Saul while he was unaware, but David refused. Instead he shared with Saul how he could have killed him but because he was a good man, he did not. Instead, he said to Saul, "May the Lord judge between you and me. And may the

Lord avenge the wrongs you have done to me, but my hand will not touch you. As the old saying goes, 'From evildoers come evil deeds,' so my hand will not touch you. Against whom has the king of Israel come out? Who are you pursuing? A dead dog? A flea? May the Lord be our judge and decide between us. May he consider my cause and uphold it; may he vindicate me by delivering me from your hand." [16] Then David promised Saul that he would never harm any of Saul's children.

We each have a special purpose in life. If we are doing the will of God, we can know that our enemies are also the enemies of God, and that God will indeed protect us from all hurt, harm, or danger.

When we are asked, where is our God? We know that we know what we know and can respond in great confidence. We will say of the Lord, "Do not take revenge, my dear friends, but leave room for God's wrath, for it is written: "It is mine to avenge; I will repay," says the Lord." [17]

Prayer

Most Gracious and Heavenly Father,

Let us be strong in the Lord and in his mighty power. For we put on the full armor of God, so that we can take our stand against the devil's schemes. For our struggle is not against flesh and blood, but against the rulers, against the authorities, against the powers of this dark world and against the spiritual forces of evil in the heavenly realms. Therefore, we put on the full armor of God, so that when the day of evil comes, we may be able to stand our ground, and after we have done everything, to stand. We stand firm then, with the belt of truth buckled around our waist, with the breastplate of righteousness in place, and with our feet fitted with the readiness that comes from the gospel of peace. In addition to all this, we take up the shield of faith, with which we can extinguish all the flaming arrows of the evil one. We take the helmet of salvation and the sword of the Spirit, which is the word of God. And we pray in the Spirit on all occasions with all kinds of prayers and requests. With this in mind, we are alert and always keep on praying for all the Lord's people. [(18)]

In Jesus' Name,
Amen

After the Storm

Then He said, "Go out, and stand on the mountain before the Lord." And behold, the Lord passed by, and a great and strong wind tore into the mountains and broke the rocks in pieces before the Lord, but the Lord was not in the wind; and after the wind an earthquake, but the Lord was not in the earthquake; and after the earthquake a fire, but the Lord was not in the fire; and after the fire a still small voice.

So it was, when Elijah heard it, that he wrapped his face in his mantle and went out and stood in the entrance of the cave. Suddenly a voice came to him, and said, "What are you doing here, Elijah?"

I Kings 19:11-13

Have you ever been in a fight? Whether it is verbal or physical, a battle can wear you out. After the dust settles, and you can get some rest, reflection begins. Depending on who you are, you will either see every victorious moment or every moment of defeat. We are all optimists or pessimists at heart. The pendulum rarely rests in the middle.

Elijah had just won an arduous battle for the Lord. The Israelites had begun worshipping the gods of the land and were no longer worshipping God. Elijah challenged all of Baal's prophets to call upon their god and he would call upon his and all would witness which would show up.

After an unsuccessful attempt by Baal's prophets and a very successful and impressive attempt by Elijah to prove that the God of Israel was real, Elijah had all of Baal's prophets executed. When Jezebel heard about their execution, she vowed to kill Elijah the next day.

Elijah fled. When he finally got a safe distance away and gave himself permission to rest, his mind was weary. He prayed for God to take his life. When he awoke, there was an angel at his side insisting for him to eat because he would have a tough journey ahead. He did as she instructed and then traveled forty days and forty nights. When he arrived at the mountain of God, he entered a cave and lamented because he was alone and his life was at risk.

God responded to his cry and promised to pass by if he went outside. After many wondrous events - strong winds, an earthquake and fire, God revealed himself in the tranquil peace of quietness and calm as a still small voice. Then God questioned Elijah.

Elijah shared that he felt alone on the battlefield for the Lord and that his life was in danger. He did not know that God had many more followers available and some whom he would instruct Elijah to anoint for his purpose. God promised Elijah that there was a succession of men who would ensure the enemies of God were destroyed. Then he provided Elijah with a mentee that would one day receive his anointing.

God knows that we are facing battles that at times can wear us down and wear us out. He is aware that we may need encouragement, strength, and help to continue the path he has called us to. We are not alone. In fact, we have everything in God. He will provide for our every need. God is not in the storm, and he is with us every step of the way with peace, security, and love.

When we are asked, where is our God? We know that we know what we know and can respond in great confidence. We will say to the Lord, "Lord God of Abraham, Isaac, and Israel, let it be known this day that You are God in Israel and I am Your servant, and that I have done all these things at Your word. Hear me, O Lord, hear me, that this people may know that You are the Lord God, and that You have turned their hearts back to You again."[19]

Prayer

Most Gracious and Heavenly Father,

Give unto the Lord, O you mighty ones. Give unto the Lord glory and strength. Give unto the Lord the glory due to His name. Worship the Lord in the beauty of holiness. The voice of the Lord is over the waters. The God of glory thunders. The Lord is over many waters. The voice of the Lord is powerful. The voice of the Lord is full of majesty. The voice of the Lord breaks the cedars. Yes, the Lord splinters the cedars of Lebanon. He makes them also skip like a calf, Lebanon and Sirion like a young wild ox. The voice of the Lord divides the flames of fire. The voice of the Lord shakes the wilderness. The Lord shakes the Wilderness of Kadesh. The voice of the Lord makes the deer give birth and strips the forests bare and in His temple everyone says, "Glory!" The Lord sat enthroned at the Flood, and the Lord sits as King forever. The Lord will give strength to His people. The Lord will bless His people with peace.[20]

In Jesus' Name,
Amen

The Audacity to Dream

"Here comes that dreamer!" they said to each other. "Come now, let's kill him and throw him into one of these cisterns and say that a ferocious animal devoured him. Then we'll see what comes of his dreams."

Genesis 37:19-20

God blesses us with unmerited favor and grants us supernatural wisdom and discernment. These blessings are not hidden from those who do not worship or honor God. Instead, they shine brightly inciting admiration or jealousy. For those who are jealous, they don't believe you have the right to desire more. It makes them uncomfortable to consider you becoming greater or gaining opportunity and growth. But God desires for us to keep dreaming, even if we don't see our dreams come to pass immediately. We are to never lose hope and embrace the audacity to dream. Just as God tells us to come boldly to the throne to seek help when we need it, we are to chase our dreams with the same boldness and tenacity that is required to achieve them.

Joseph was born late in his father's life to the wife

he loved most, therefore he was granted unmerited favor. His older brothers took notice and could not find a kind word to say to him because they were jealous. Joseph was naive to the fact that he was treated differently and never minced words when it came to reporting his brother's nefarious activities or sharing his bold dreams. Joseph's behavior infuriated his siblings even more.

One day, Joseph was tasked with locating his brothers and reporting to his father on how things were going. He left home in a fine coat of many colors that his father had created for him, and it was unlike anything any of his brother's owned. When he arrived where they should have been, the brothers had already moved to a new location. Fortunately, a stranger saw them and reported to Joseph what he heard. Joseph went after them.

His brothers saw him coming from afar off and plotted to kill him. They were tired of him and wanted to be rid of his presence for good. But his older brother Reuben knew this would not be good and that there would be nothing they could tell their father if he did not return. Another brother Judah suggested they throw him into an empty water tank. When Joseph arrived, that is exactly what they did. They snatched the coat off him and threw him down into the empty tank.

As they ate, a group of Ishmaelites (descendants of their great uncle Ishmael) were headed to Egypt with items they hoped to sell. The brothers wanted to be rid of Joseph, so they sold him as a slave to the traveling men. They then took Joseph's coat, dipped in the blood of a goat they slaughtered and convinced their father that he was dead. Their father vowed to mourn Joseph for as long as he lived.

For many years, Joseph served many masters with excellence. He always had a good attitude and disposition and was always willing to help. Unfortunately, time and time again, his kindness was met with unfair treatment and accusations. Until one day, about 13 years later, he was given an opportunity to interpret a dream of Pharaoh. Not only was he able to interpret the dream, he was also able to provide Pharaoh with a plan that would bless Egypt and the surrounding countries.

When the famine hit the area, it was debilitating to every country except Egypt because of Joseph's plan. His family back home was starving and the same brothers that sold him into slavery were forced to travel to Egypt to try and buy food. When they arrived, they had no idea they were speaking to the brother they wanted to kill and treated so badly.

Rather than deny them or refuse to bless them, Joseph forgave them as all his audacious dreams had finally come true. Joseph blessed his family to relocate to Egypt and they were able to live a comfortable life thanks to his ability to achieve what he dreamed he could. His journey was not easy but because he trusted God to deliver him, he made it to the other side and was blessed for not giving up.

We are to always have the audacity to dream. The desires in our hearts were placed there by God. He has already designed our destination and is guiding us along our path. Despite any opposition we may face, any discouragement we may experience, or setbacks that push us to give up, we must continue and move forward. God is not a man that he should tell a lie. If he promised us we would become greater, he is preparing us to do just that.

When we are asked, where is our God? We know that we know what we know and can respond in great confidence. We will say of the Lord, "We do not fret because of evil men or be envious of those who do wrong; for like the grass they will soon wither, like green plants they will soon die away. We will trust in the LORD and do good; dwell in the land and enjoy safe pasture. We will delight ourselves in the LORD and he will give us the desires of our hearts. We will commit our ways to the LORD; and trust in him and he will do this: He will make our righteousness shine like the dawn, the justice of our cause like the noonday sun. We will be still before the LORD and wait patiently for him. We will not fret when men succeed in their ways, when they carry out their wicked schemes. We will refrain from anger and turn from wrath; we will not fret--it leads only to evil. For evil men will be cut off, but those who hope in the LORD will inherit the land." [21]

Prayer

Most Gracious and Heavenly Father,

You, God, are our God, earnestly we seek you; we thirst for you, our whole being longs for you, in a dry and parched land where there is no water. We have seen you in the sanctuary and beheld your power and your glory. Because your love is better than life, our lips will glorify you. We will praise you as long as we live, and in your name we will lift up our hands. We will be fully satisfied as with the richest of foods; with singing lips our mouths will praise you. On our beds we remember you; we think of you through the watches of the night. Because you are our help, we sing in the shadow of your wings. We cling to you; your right hand upholds us. Those who want to kill us will be destroyed; they will go down to the depths of the earth. They will be given over to the sword and become food for jackals. But the king will rejoice in God; all who swear by God will glory in him, while the mouths of liars will be silenced. [22]

In Jesus' Name,
Amen

God is Doing a New Thing

He said to them, "I see that your father's attitude toward me is not what it was before, but the God of my father has been with me. You know that I've worked for your father with all my strength, yet your father has cheated me by changing my wages ten times. However, God has not allowed him to harm me.

Genesis 31:6-7

Injustice can sometimes go on for much longer than anyone suffering would expect. The ancestors of African-American slaves had no idea that their captivity and torture would last for over 400 years. When we are experiencing hardship, we want it to end quickly, but sometimes God allows us to suffer for much longer than we imagine possible. Nelson Mandela spent twenty-seven years in prison before being released and rose to ultimate power as the president of South Africa. His political fight against apartheid caused him to endure incredible hardships.

So many in the Bible suffered at the hands of those in power, Jacob was no different. After cheating his own brother out of his birthright, Jacob fell in love with the most beautiful woman he'd ever met. He promised her father he would work seven long years to take her hand in marriage. However, on his wedding night, her father cheated Jacob and caused him to marry her older and less attractive sister instead. But Jacob loved the younger sister, so he agreed to work for seven more years to take her hand in marriage. After marrying the younger sister, their father asked Jacob to stay and help tend his flocks. Again, Jacob agreed and stayed even longer. Finally, Jacob asked for what he felt was a fair wage and asked to receive all of the spotted or striped flocks (being that at any moment his flocks could be checked and easily identified as his own). His wives' father agreed but soon became disgusted with Jacob and treated him as though he was unwanted.

Jacob could not believe that after all the blessings he'd bestowed on their father that he would treat Jacob in such a manner. Even his brothers-in-law accused Jacob of wrongdoing. That is when Jacob heard from God that it was time to go home. God promised to be with him. God also gave Jacob supernatural wisdom and discernment because God saw all that his father-in-law had done to Jacob.

Jacob knew that if he told Laban, his father-in-law that he was leaving, that he would try to take his wives, servant wives, children and possibly his flocks from him. So he snuck away in the middle of the night.

Rachel, Jacob's most beloved wife, stole a spiritual idol from her father and caused him to fly into a rage. Laban hunted Jacob and his family down. Once he caught up with them, he accused Jacob and shared his anger at their sneaking away and stealing from him. But Jacob denied taking anything from the man and allowed him to search everything and everywhere. Rachel had hidden the god and was sitting on it so that it was never found.

Her father claimed that he could have caused Jacob harm but would not have done anything at all to Jacob, still he accused him of taking all that belonged to him. Laban explained to Jacob that God had come to him in a dream and warned him not to say a word to Jacob (whether good or bad). Jacob rebutted. He insisted that had God not been on his side and rebuked Laban, he knew that his father-in-law would have never allowed him to return home with all that he'd rightfully earned.

That day Laban and Jacob made a pact to serve as a witness between them signifying a promise not to harm one another from that day moving forward. Laban also made Jacob promise to not harm his daughters or grandchildren.

No matter how long we have been oppressed or mistreated, God will protect us. He will shut the mouths of our enemies and force them to release us from servitude. God is sovereign and he is in control. God is doing a new thing. Jacob not only left with far more than he arrived with, he was blessed to become a father to the twelve tribes of Israel. God wrestled with Jacob throughout the night and blessed him as a man that wrestled with God and man and won.

When we are asked, where is our God? We know that we know what we know and can respond in great confidence. We will say of the Lord, "It is he who made a way through the sea, a path through the mighty waters, who drew out the chariots and horses, the army and reinforcements together, and they lay there, never to rise again, extinguished, snuffed out like a wick. We forget the former things; we do not dwell on the past. See, God is doing a new thing! Now it springs up; do we not perceive it? God is making a way in the wilderness and streams in the wasteland. The wild animals honor Him, the jackals and the owls, because He provides water in the wilderness and streams in the wasteland, to give drink to His people, His chosen, the people He formed for Himself that we may proclaim His praise." [23]

Prayer

Most Gracious and Heavenly Father,

You are he who created Jacob, and he who formed Israel: We will not fear, for you have redeemed us. You have summoned us by name; we belong to you. When we pass through the waters, you will be with us, and when we pass through the rivers, they will not sweep over us. When we walk through the fire, we will not be burned; the flames will not set us ablaze. For you are the Lord our God, the Holy One of Israel, our Savior; you give Egypt for our ransom, Cush and Seba in your stead. Since we are precious and honored in your sight, and because you love us, you will give people in exchange for us, nations in exchange for our life. We will not be afraid, for you are with us; you will bring our children from the east and gather us from the west.
You will say to the north, 'Give them up!' and to the south, 'Do not hold them back. Bring my sons from afar and my daughters from the ends of the earth—everyone who is called by my name, whom I created for my glory, whom I formed and made." [24]

In Jesus' Name,
Amen

Supernatural Blessings

Then the Lord said to Joshua, "See, I have delivered Jericho into your hands, along with its king and its fighting men.

Joshua 6:2

God is so good that he fights every battle for us. We don't have to fight, all we have to do is show up and obey. The enemy that we see today is already defeated.

While the enemy is watching us and devising a plot to destroy us, God is behind the scenes making sure that no weapon formed against us can prosper. What they meant was for evil, but God has meant it for good. In fact, it was God who designed that season of opposition as a set up to grant us victory despite adverse circumstances. He wanted to show the enemy that he could trust us to obey him even when everything looked dark and dismal.

Victory belongs to us.

We can't be surprised when Satan does what he is expected to do - steal, kill and destroy. We must remember that it is not flesh and blood we are up against, but principalities of evil. God is no respecter of persons. Instead of focusing on our enemies, we need to be paying attention to what God is doing.

Joshua led the Israelites after the death of Moses. He was a man of God and sought God for direction and guidance. His army was made up of young men, not the same men that travelled out of Egypt, but these men were born in the wilderness or during the journey into the wilderness. They hadn't yet been circumcised. Once they were circumcised (by God's command), God released blessings on the people of Israel. No longer did they receive manna, but they began to experience the blessings of the land of Canaan.

At the same time, the Ammonites and Canaanites feared the people of God because of what happened to Pharaoh's army. So much so they'd locked the gates of Jericho keeping Joshua and his army out, and the people of Jericho in. It was locked up tight with all the fighting men, right behind the walls.

Then an angel of the Lord appeared. He told Joshua the land he stood on was holy and that he was neither an enemy nor a supporter of Israel. Joshua bowed in humility and asked the angel to share the message God had for him.

God gave Joshua detailed instructions on how to defeat Jericho. He and the army, priests and people followed those instructions to the letter. The walls of the city simply fell at their feet because they obeyed God. Then they went in and destroyed every living thing, except for Rahab, who'd honored God by protecting his people.

God's instructions did not sound natural. It did

not make sense for Joshua and his army to do what they did, but obedience and trust in God was at the center of their victory. Sometimes God will ask us to do something that doesn't make sense, but God is in the process of making every crooked place straight. We don't know how walking around the walls of Jericho made them fall. We don't know how not saying a word until the seventh day and shouting made the difference. All we know is that when they did what God told them to do, they were granted full access to the blessing.

When we are asked, where is our God? We know that we know what we know and can respond in great confidence. We will say of the Lord, "God will repay us for the years the locusts have eaten—the great locust and the young locust, the other locusts and the locust swarm—his great army that he sent among us. We will have plenty to eat, until we are full, and we will praise the name of the Lord our God, who has worked wonders for us; never again will we be shamed. Then we will know that God is in Israel, that he is the Lord our God, and that there is no other; never again will we be shamed."[25]

Prayer

Most Gracious and Heavenly Father,

You are our portion, LORD; we have promised to obey your words. We have sought your face with all our hearts; be gracious to us according to your promise. We have considered our ways and have turned our steps to your statutes. We will hasten and not delay to obey your commands. Though the wicked bind us with ropes, we will not forget your law. At midnight we rise to give you thanks for your righteous laws. We are a friend to all who fear you, to all who follow your precepts. The earth is filled with your love, LORD; teach us your decrees. [26]

In Jesus' Name,
Amen

Songs in the Night

I remembered you, God, and I groaned; I meditated, and my spirit grew faint.

Psalm 77:3

The darkest days of my life were days when I was homeless with children, or jarringly poor to the point of not being able to provide them with food, shelter, water, and electricity. There were other dark moments, like those of being addicted to drugs, and my own homelessness, but none were quite as difficult as the nights alone staring at my children and realizing there was no solution in sight.

Job was a father, a business owner, a husband, and friend. When his life began to fall apart, he lost all of what mattered most, barring his relationship with God. He lost his children, his livelihood, the comforting support of his wife and the unquestionable respect of his friends.

Satan wanted to prove that a man that loses all he has will almost certainly lose his faith. But God knew better because he could see the integrity and motive within Job's heart.

Job's wife and friends challenged him. His wife told him to curse God and die. His friends accused him of secret sin. Job himself prayed for God to let him die, because he had nothing to hope for and nothing to look forward to. He and his friends wondered... Where was God? They in fact, stated many times over, if God were here, I would ask... and the questions loomed on. Until one day, Job heard from God.

God asked him if he was there when God formed the earth, the stars, the galaxy, and all it contained. He asked him many questions to help Job realize that he was a man, a finite being with limited power. He also told Job that his friends were wrong to accuse him and he told Job to pray for them. Job did.

After a season, everything he lost was restored. In fact, he received double of everything he lost. The point of the matter is that all we go through God has allowed. Our seasons of loss, pain, and difficulty help shape us into who we are today and who God needs us to be tomorrow. Everything is connected and God is intentional.

When we are asked, where is our God? We know that we know what we know and can respond in great confidence. We will say of the Lord, "God is our maker, who gives songs in the night, who teaches us more than he teaches the beasts of the earth and makes us wiser than the birds in the sky. For the Lord takes delight in his people; he crowns the humble with victory. Let his faithful people rejoice in this honor and sing for joy on their beds. May the praise of God be in our mouths and a double-edged sword in our hands, to inflict vengeance on the nations and punishment on the peoples, to bind their kings with fetters, their nobles with shackles of iron, to carry out the sentence written against them—this is the glory of all his faithful people."[27]

Prayer

Most Gracious and Heavenly Father,

May those who seek our lives be disgraced and put to shame; may those who plot our ruin be turned back in dismay. May they be like chaff before the wind, with the angel of the Lord driving them away; may their path be dark and slippery, with the angel of the Lord pursuing them. Since they hid their net for us without cause and without cause dug a pit for us, may ruin overtake them by surprise—may the net they hid entangle them, may they fall into the pit, to their ruin. Then our souls will rejoice in the Lord and delight in his salvation. Our whole being will exclaim, "Who is like you, Lord? You rescue the poor from those too strong for them, the poor and needy from those who rob them."[28]

In Jesus' Name,
Amen

Trusting God

These are the nations the Lord left to test all those Israelites who had not experienced any of the wars in Canaan (he did this only to teach warfare to the descendants of the Israelites who had not had previous battle experience): the five rulers of the Philistines, all the Canaanites, the Sidonians, and the Hivites living in the Lebanon mountains from Mount Baal Hermon to Lebo Hamath. They were left to test the Israelites to see whether they would obey the Lord's commands, which he had given their ancestors through Moses.

Judges 3:1-4

Adversity toughens us for what is ahead. The battles we face are meant to make us strong. Our goal is to walk in obedience during the test to ensure that God will direct us and prepare us for battle. Tests also strengthen our relationship with God by developing trust, dependence, and confidence when we need it most.

After many battles with many nations involving various groups of Israelites, the battle between Barak, leader of the Israelite army and Sisera, leader of the Canaanite army will always be remembered because of the lack of confidence Barak had in his ability to conquer the king's army.

After being oppressed by Canaan for more than twenty years, the cry of God's people was answered.

Deborah, a prophet and current leader of Israel predicted that Barak would return with victory after a battle against Sisera. Sisera's army was no less than magnificent and strong, with more than 900 chariots fitted with iron. Despite the positive prophecy, Barak refused to go without the prophet by his side. Deborah promised to go but told Barak because he lacked the confidence to go in his own strength with faith in God, the victory would be attributed to a woman.

Barak's army faced off against Sisera's army and bitterly defeated every one of Sisera's warriors, leading them to death. Sisera was the lone survivor of the battle and managed to make it to the tent of an Israelite family sojourning in Canaan, who had won the favor of the king and was considered a friend of the king of Canaan.

Sisera trusted Jael, the woman of the house. She offered him safety and comfort. She promised to persuade his enemies he was not in her tent when they came by to look for him. But just as the leader of the Canaanite army let his guard down and fell fast asleep, she struck him through the temple with a large stake and hammer. He died instantly. When Barak, head of the Israelite army came searching, she revealed the dead man's carcass to him.

God will grant us the ability to accomplish his every desire. He expects us to move and do what he has asked in faith, trusting and believing that he will come through. When we give our responsibilities to others or let others dictate to us what should be done, we are granting our victory to them.

When we are asked, where is our God? We know that we know what we know and can respond in great confidence. We will say of the Lord, "God chose new leaders when war came to the city gates, but not a shield or spear was seen among forty thousand in Israel. My heart is with Israel's princes, with the willing volunteers among the people. Praise the Lord! " [29]

Prayer

Most Gracious and Heavenly Father,

May all your enemies perish, Lord! But may all who love you be like the sun when it rises in its strength. [30] *Blessed are they who trust in the Lord, who do not look to the proud, to those who turn aside to false gods. Many, Lord our God, are the wonders you have done, the things you planned for us. None can compare with you; were we to speak and tell of your deeds, they would be too many to declare. Sacrifice and offering you did not desire—but my ears you have opened—burnt offerings and sin offerings you did not require. Then we said, "Here we are, we have come—it is written about us in the scroll. We desire to do your will, our God; your law is within our hearts. We proclaim your saving acts in the great assembly; we do not seal our lips, Lord, as you know. We do not hide your righteousness in our hearts; we speak of your faithfulness and your saving help. We do not conceal your love and your faithfulness from the great assembly. Do not withhold your mercy from us, Lord; may your love and faithfulness always protect us. For troubles without number surround us; our sins have overtaken us, and we cannot see. They are more than the hairs of our head, and our hearts fail within us. Be pleased to save us, Lord; come quickly, Lord, to help us.* [31]

In Jesus' Name,
Amen

Forever & Always

Posterity will serve him; future generations will be told about the Lord. They will proclaim his righteousness, declaring to a people yet unborn: He has done it!

Psalm 22:30-31

As Christians, we have learned through revelation and relationship that Jesus is real. Generations of people before us and after us have learned and will learn of Christ, but our experience with Christ begins the day he chooses to reveal himself to us. In that moment, at that time, we know him and more importantly, we recognize that he truly knows us.

David penned Psalm 22 more than 1,000 years before Christ walked the earth. While much of what David says in the psalm can be attributed to his personal sufferings as he was chased by King Saul, fighting with Absalom, or on the battlefield, amazingly, David was prophesying the crucifixion of Jesus Christ and the legacy he would leave on the earth.

From the anguish he felt in Gethsemane, to the

nails piercing his hands and feet, to the men gambling over his clothing, to the pointing fingers and mocking words of those who watched him die and refused to believe that he was doing the work of God, Jesus suffered that we may live.

David also recognizes and reiterates a consistent theme throughout the text. He shares that he learned of God through his ancestors, who believed and trusted in the Lord and the Lord delivered them. As a believer, even though he is suffering, his faith is in the Lord, and vows to give him praise. He insists that all give him praise. Finally, he shares that all future generations (posterity) will serve the Lord, and that future generations would be told about him. There is a recurring theme throughout the text that the knowledge and service of Christ will be extended and available to all.

We overcome by the power of our testimony. Nothing is known of what was before without someone sharing the story or documenting the process. We must share with our children and their children about the goodness of the Lord. We must be willing to show them how God impacted and changed our lives. We must be willing to document through memorials the act of worship to God. This is how we are strengthened, encouraged, and refreshed during hard times. We can look back and remember how God was with us before, he will surely be with us again.

When we are asked, where is our God? We know that we know what we know and can respond in great confidence. We will say of the Lord, "Even though we walk through the darkest valley, we will fear no evil, for you are with us; your rod and your staff, they comfort us." [32]

Prayer

Most Gracious and Heavenly Father,

In the future, when our sons ask us, "What is the meaning of the stipulations, decrees and laws the Lord our God has commanded you?" We will tell them: "We were slaves of Pharaoh in Egypt, but the Lord brought us out of Egypt with a mighty hand. Before our eyes the Lord sent signs and wonders—great and terrible—on Egypt and Pharaoh and his whole household. But he brought us out from there to bring us in and give us the land he promised on oath to our ancestors. The Lord commanded us to obey all these decrees and to fear the Lord our God, so that we might always prosper and be kept alive, as is the case today. And if we are careful to obey all this law before the Lord our God, as he has commanded us, that will be our righteousness". [33]

In Jesus' Name,
Amen

Blessed by God

"Lord," Ananias answered, "I have heard many reports about this man and all the harm he has done to your holy people in Jerusalem. And he has come here with authority from the chief priests to arrest all who call on your name."

Acts 9:13-14

The enemy may plot an untimely death for you, but God will grant you favor, wisdom, and discernment. When God has decided to bless you, nothing can block his blessing. What is for you is for you. No one can take it away. The enemy can try, but if he isn't careful, he may find himself subjected to the ultimate will of God and be used to facilitate a blessing he tried to block.

After the death of Stephen, Saul realized it was the perfect opportunity to gather the followers of Jesus and persecute them all. But God, who knew the plot of Saul, struck him blind before he could arrive. Saul sat blind and dumbfounded for three days without food or drink. He prayed.

Then God told a faithful servant to go and retrieve

Saul and restore his sight. Ananias knew the reputation and purpose of Saul's visit and was uncertain of his assignment. But God insisted he go and do as he was told. Ananias obeyed God and restored Saul's sight. The Christians he'd come to persecute were instead blessed with peace and strength.

Saul in his conversion became Paul and witnessed for Jesus helping many to believe. The Jews devised a plan to kill him, but Paul learned of their plot and was protected by God.

Meanwhile, Peter was performing miracles, healing the ill in Lydda when a beautiful woman of God fell sick and died in the neighboring town of Joppa. Many loved her because she was a good woman who served others with gladness. So, when some of the men from town heard that Peter was healing a town away, they traveled to get him. When Peter arrived, the dead woman laid in an upstairs bedroom surrounded by women who'd loved her and were grateful for her. Peter sent them from the room and prayed, then he commanded her to rise. She did. This miracle was heard of throughout the town leading many to come and be healed by Peter.

No matter what, we must believe and know that God is always for us. When Saul tried to bring terror and destruction to the followers of Christ, God converted him to become a follower of Christ that would face great persecution. When the enemy tried to strike fear into the heart of Ananias and convince him that his enemy would destroy him, God allowed him to stand before him boldly with power, restoring his sight and witnessing his helplessness under the power of God. When the enemy tried to take the life of a woman whose sole commitment was to bring love and life to others, God turned it around giving her life back and using the miracle to bring even more life to those who would believe in God because of her miracle.

The enemy thinks he is smart, but God is all knowing, all powerful and sovereign.

When we are asked, where is our God? We know that we know what we know and can respond in great confidence. We will say of the Lord, "No weapon forged against us will prevail, and we will refute every tongue that accuses us. This is the heritage of the servants of the LORD, and this is our vindication from him." [(34)]

Prayer

Most Gracious and Heavenly Father,

The Lord is our refuge and we make the Most High our dwelling, no harm will overtake us, no disaster will come near our tent. For the Lord will command his angels concerning us to guard us in all our ways; they will lift us up in their hands, so that we will not strike our foot against a stone. We will tread on the lion and the cobra; we will trample the great lion and the serpent. "Because they love me," says the Lord, "I will rescue them; I will protect them, for they acknowledge my name. They will call on me, and I will answer them; I will be with them in trouble, I will deliver them and honor them. With long life I will satisfy them and show them my salvation." [(35)]

In Jesus' Name,
Amen

Never Again

The Lord smelled the pleasing aroma and said in his heart: "Never again will I curse the ground because of humans, even though every inclination of the human heart is evil from childhood. And never again will I destroy all living creatures, as I have done.

Genesis 8:21

Our decisions have destinations. When we make decisions that cause us great pain, through experience we learn what makes us uncomfortable and then we pivot or choose a different route. Occasionally, we are required to sit in a decision we have made for a while so that we may value the loss we suffer with clarity and truth. This can be especially poignant when it concerns anything we create, birth, or help to become. Our greatest desire is to see our image of self-reflection in all that we are willing to invest our time, attention and resources to. But when that reflection is not what we hope, we must go back to the drawing board and define a different path.

Adam and his immediate descendants lived for

a very long time, on average between 900 years of age and 969 years of age. But as time went on the sons of God (fallen angels) began to have children with the daughters of man (humans). The decision of the sons of God to procreate with the daughters of man caused God to decide about man that would greatly reduce their lifespan to become only 25% of what it once was.

Sin and violence were prevalent in all humans, so much so that it deeply saddened God and he regretted making man. [(37)]

But Noah was a blameless man that worshiped God daily. He found favor in the sight of God and was commissioned to save humanity and the world. In order to do so, God asked Noah to do what to others may have seemed unreasonable, unnecessary, and unwarranted. But rather than question God, Noah walked by faith. In fact, when Noah was born his father Lamech prophesied over Noah when he named him saying, “This one will bring us relief from the agonizing labor of our hands, caused by the ground the Lord has cursed.” [(36)]

When the day of destruction arrived, Noah and his family were safe inside the ark. Pairs of every animal and bird God told Noah to bring survived. They were protected from the storm because Noah obeyed God even when all he had was a word from God. Noah did not receive confirmation by way of a weather report, prophet or other. He simply heard God tell him what to do. Mind you, Noah’s ark was no ordinary boat, it required Noah to adhere to every specificity of wood type, mortar, and measurement of each area.

After forty days of non-stop water pressure (rain and spigots erupting from the ground), God’s storm surged and purged every living thing from the face of the earth which itself was completely covered in water. No living thing that required breath could withstand the storm.

When God destroyed the earth and all living creatures because of the continual and violent sin of men, he vowed never to do it again. All living beings (plants, animals, and humans) breathe the air of the earth and require air to live. When God destroyed the earth, he took his breath away from every living creature... except those in the ark.

Ever since the fall of Adam and Eve the earth was cursed. Evil resides within man and only the spirit of God can replace it. We are mortal beings, and our earthly nature will expire but the spirit God replaces our earthly spirit with will live forever, if we accept it.

At that time, Noah was the only man found willing to fully embrace the spirit of God. Not only did he walk with him, but he also allowed God to lead him. In this, Noah found favor with God and therefore saved humanity. All God needed was one man, he didn't need an army. With one man, he saved humanity. With one man, he saved us from sin. God's spirit will always reign no matter how dark it gets or no matter the amount of evil we see. The Spirit of God is sovereign, present, and the only authority over the earth.

Our decisions have destinations. Whether that destination is a place we desire can only be determined over time. When God moves, we move. God decided to destroy the earth, so that we would have an opportunity to experience and appreciate his love, mercy, and grace. Noah decided to listen, trust, and obey God, leading to a destination filled with a people who knew the name of God and allowed his spirit to reign within them. If we are walking in the will of God, our decisions are a part of God's plan.

Never again will God destroy the earth because we have elected to welcome his spirit into our beings. We walk with God and we obey his command. We embrace a nevertheless thy will be done lifestyle and choose life that it may be well with us and our descendants. We are those who can open the door of truth for those who do not know God. When we are asked, where is our God? We know that we know what we know and can respond in great confidence. We will say of the Lord, "As long as the earth endures, seedtime and harvest, cold and heat, summer and winter, day and night will never cease." [38]

Prayer

Most Gracious and Heavenly Father,

Praise the Lord, our souls. Lord our God, you are very great; you are clothed with splendor and majesty. The Lord wraps himself in light as with a garment; he stretches out the heavens like a tent and lays the beams of his upper chambers on their waters. He makes the clouds his chariot and rides on the wings of the wind. He makes winds his messengers, flames of fire his servants. He set the earth on its foundations; it can never be moved. You covered it with the watery depths as with a garment; the waters stood above the mountains. But at your rebuke the waters fled, at the sound of your thunder they took to flight; they flowed over the mountains, they went down into the valleys, to the place you assigned for them. You set a boundary they cannot cross; never again will they cover the earth. [39]

In Jesus' Name,
Amen

In Your Hands

"He is in your hands," King Zedekiah answered. "The king can do nothing to oppose you."

Jeremiah 38:5

Your confidence and presence can be perceived as a threat to some. Especially when you are courageous, brave, and unafraid to speak the truth to power. Political leaders like Martin Luther King, Jr., Malcolm X, Fred Hampton, and many others have been murdered for leading a group in opposition of the government. In the same way, we are called as Christians to step up and say what God tells us to say, whether it is comfortable for us to do so or not. When we are obedient in this way, we can incite a level of anger that may threaten our safety and our livelihood.

Jeremiah was a prophet chosen by God to reveal an uncomfortable message with urgency and clarity. The community was abuzz and local government leaders heard what Jeremiah was saying and reported it to the king. In their report, they insisted that Jeremiah must die for what he has done. The king relented and gave them permission to do as they saw fit.

The leaders had Jeremiah wrangled and wrought him into an empty cistern filled with mud. Their goal was to allow him to starve to death, alone, with no one to help. But a local official saw what had been done and reported the matter to the king. The king told the young man to go and rescue Jeremiah, and to take thirty men with him to ensure he was successful. They rescued Jeremiah and gave him a safer place to stay.

Then the king sent for Jeremiah and asked him to share God's message with him. Jeremiah was hesitant as the king had just permitted his leadership to kill him. The king promised that he would not hurt Jeremiah. Jeremiah told the king that if he did not obey God and submit himself to the King of Babylon, then the city would be burned, and he and his family would surely die. But if he did obey, he had no one to fear and all would go well for him. Furthermore, if he elected not to do as God said, he would be taunted for being tricked by the words of his leadership as a man whose feet have been stuck in the mud.

Then the king told Jeremiah to keep their conversation quiet and to tell those who may question him that he was simply pleading for his life. Otherwise, the men would kill Jeremiah for sharing such a message with the king. Jeremiah did what the king asked and was safe.

When we are asked, where is our God? We know that we know what we know and can respond in great confidence. We will say of the Lord, "All who take refuge in you are glad; they always sing for joy. Spread your protection over them, that those who love your name may rejoice in you." [(40)]

Prayer

Most Gracious and Heavenly Father,

We confidently say of our enemies and all who wish us harm, "Away from us, all you who do evil, for the Lord has heard our weeping. The Lord has heard our cry for mercy; the Lord accepts our prayer. All of our enemies will be overwhelmed with shame and anguish; they will turn back and suddenly be put to shame." (41)

In Jesus' Name,
Amen

Anointed for Greatness

So he sent for him and had him brought in. He was glowing with health and had a fine appearance and handsome features. Then the Lord said, "Rise and anoint him; this is the one."

I Samuel 16:12

You may not realize it, but God is working behind the scenes to grant you favor and success. Your name is being spoken in rooms you have no knowledge of, and your skills have grabbed the attention of those in influence. We were all created for a unique purpose. If we keep God first, he is going to open doors that no man can shut.

David was a shepherd, minding his business and tending his sheep, when one day, a prophet of God arrived in Bethlehem. The prophet Samuel invited his father and sons to a sacrifice to worship the Lord. Samuel knew by the appearance of Jesse's sons that surely the next king was among them. But he wasn't. In fact, the one God wanted to anoint king was considered the least in the household by his father, who hadn't even invited him to join them.

Jesse then called for David, his youngest son. God told Samuel that David was the one he'd selected to become next in line as king. Samuel anointed David that day.

Meanwhile, Saul, the current king, was troubled by evil spirits and was told that only a person who could play the soothing music of a stringed instrument could console him. In that moment, a young man told the king,

"I have seen a son of Jesse of Bethlehem who knows how to play the lyre. He is a brave man and a warrior. He speaks well and is a fine-looking man. And the Lord is with him." [42]

Immediately, King Saul sent for David, and he was added to the king's service.

It doesn't matter what it looks like. You can be the least of your family, the worst dressed, disabled, or simply considered as unworthy of positions of greatness. What matters is what God sees. What God has decided to bless, no one can curse.

When we are asked, where is our God? We know that we know what we know and can respond in great confidence. We will say of the Lord, "We are His workmanship, created in Christ Jesus for good works, which God prepared beforehand so that we would walk in them." [43]

Prayer

Most Gracious and Heavenly Father,

How abundant are the good things that you have stored up for those who fear you, that you bestow in the sight of all, on those who take refuge in you. In the shelter of your presence you hide us from all human intrigues; you keep us safe in your dwelling from accusing tongues. Praise be to the Lord, for he showed us the wonders of his love when we were in a city under siege. In our alarm we said, "We are cut off from your sight!" Yet you heard our cry for mercy when we called to you for help. Love the Lord, all his faithful people! The Lord preserves those who are true to him, but the proud he pays back in full. We will be strong and take heart, yes, we hope in the Lord. [(44)]

In Jesus' Name,
Amen

Chosen

With them were Heman and Jeduthun and the rest of those chosen and designated by name to give thanks to the Lord, "for his love endures forever."

I Chronicles 16:41

Everyone wants to be chosen. It is not comfortable or delightful to try and make a place for yourself in an area where you are uninvited and unwanted. Rejection is painful for anyone. But for some, it can be debilitating.

When King David first attempted to get the ark of the covenant, one of the men carrying the ark stumbled and grabbed it to protect the ark from falling to the ground. The man was killed for doing so. This gave David great fear, and he left the ark in the home of a man by the name of Obed-Edom. Now after a time, David realized that Obed-Edom was blessed because the ark resided there.

So David prayed and asked God how to retrieve the ark. In response, David discovered that only the ministers of the Lord (the sons of Aaron and the Levites) could carry the ark. Then as they brought the ark into Jerusalem, David danced in praise!

Then he told the priests and ministers of music to praise God by giving glory to his name and thanking him for all he has done. He told them to praise God in this way:

Give praise to the Lord, proclaim his name; make known among the nations what he has done. Sing to him, sing praise to him; tell of all his wonderful acts. Glory in his holy name; let the hearts of those who seek the Lord rejoice. Look to the Lord and his strength; seek his face always. Remember the wonders he has done, his miracles, and the judgments he pronounced, you his servants, the descendants of Israel, his chosen ones, the children of Jacob. He is the Lord our God; his judgments are in all the earth. [(45)]

Just as God chose the ministers to carry the ark of the Lord, he has chosen each of us who seek him the honor of carrying the Holy Spirit within us. The ministers in the Old Testament lived holy lives that were dedicated to Christ. Likewise, we too must live holy lives dedicated to Christ.

But we are not perfect people. We sin every day, but God is a forgiving God. He has not discriminated against us, calling us unworthy. Instead, God calls us to share the goodness of the Lord with others. We are to tell of his unending mercy and how we have received undeserved grace. In our weakness is his strength made perfect. God has everything we need in him. Jesus died to be an inclusive God, calling all men unto him.

Jesus stands at the door and knocks on every person's heart. He does not change. He is the same. God is and he always will be sovereign and he deserves all the praise. We fail him daily, but God is faithful to forgive when we ask. All God asks of us is to share his good news with others that they may recognize him and be saved. We are all given the opportunity to come boldly before his throne to receive mercy while it is still available. But how will anyone else know unless we tell them? It is our responsibility to share the good news with those we know are in need of his acceptance, his love and his unyielding mercy and grace.

God has called each of us by name. He knows our condition; he knows our weaknesses. He knows everything about us. When the world has rejected us, turned their back on us because they have considered us unworthy of their attention, time, or resource, God opens a door and says, 'Welcome.' God sees what others reject and calls us mighty warriors, kings, and worthy of his adoption. Jesus himself was rejected by his own people, but God raised him up as a Savior to all.

The stone the builders rejected has become the cornerstone; the Lord has done this, and it is marvelous in our eyes. The Lord has done it this very day; let us rejoice today and be glad. [(46)]

Each of us was created to serve a unique purpose. As in the story of Queen Esther when her cousin Mordecai approached her about using her position to save the people of God, he said to her what I believe God is saying to those he has given an abundance of his mercy and grace,

"If you remain silent at this time, relief and deliverance for the (elect) will arise from another place, but you and your father's family will perish. And who knows but that you have come to your royal position for such a time as this?" [47]

When we are asked, where is our God? We know that we know what we know and can respond in great confidence. We will say of the Lord, "Ascribe to the Lord, all you families of nations, ascribe to the Lord glory and strength. Ascribe to the Lord the glory due his name; bring an offering and come before him. Worship the Lord in the splendor of his holiness." [48]

Prayer

Most Gracious and Heavenly Father,

Let all tremble before you, all the earth! The world is firmly established; it cannot be moved. Let the heavens rejoice, let the earth be glad; let them say among the nations, "The Lord reigns!" Let the sea resound, and all that is in it; let the fields be jubilant, and everything in them! Let the trees of the forest sing, let them sing for joy before the Lord, for he comes to judge the earth. Give thanks to the Lord, for he is good; his love endures forever. Cry out, "Save us, God our Savior; gather us and deliver us from the nations, that we may give thanks to your holy name, and glory in your praise. Praise be to the Lord, the God of Israel, from everlasting to everlasting. Let all the people say "Amen" and "Praise the Lord. [49]

In Jesus Name,
Amen

A Reckless Path

When Balaam looked out and saw Israel encamped tribe by tribe, the Spirit of God came on him.

Numbers 24:2

As children of God, our reputation will proceed us. People will seek us out for our gifts. We must be certain that as we walk with God, we are doing the will of God at all times. It is our responsibility to stay above influence to clearly ascertain our role and responsibility, especially as new opportunities arise.

The prophet Balaam was known to speak the Word of God and people would often seek his counsel. The Israelites were doing just as God had promised them as they left Egypt with Moses. They were conquering the nations in their promised land that God had provided to them as an inheritance.

When Balak, the King of Moab saw the Israelites outside his territory, he immediately called on Balaam, the prophet of God to pronounce a curse on the Israelites to prevent them from conquering his land. He was filled with dread and summoned Balaam to come immediately. He even sent a fee for the divination.

But God came to Balaam and told him he could not curse what God has blessed. Balaam informed the men from Moab of what God shared and sent them on their way.

Then Balak sent a bigger group with men that held greater honor. He told them to tell Balaam not to allow anything to stop him from coming and that he would reward Balaam handsomely if he could only come to bless his kingdom. He also shared that he would do whatever Balaam told him to do.

God told Balaam to go with the men the next morning but to only say what God told him to say. Balaam got up the next morning and started on his way. But God was very angry. He sent an angel to block the journey of Balaam as he rode his donkey. Balaam could not see the angel but the donkey could. Every time the donkey tried to avoid the angel; Balaam would beat the donkey.

God opened the mouth of the donkey and the donkey questioned Balaam's actions, citing his past performance as evidence of his good character. Then God opened Balaam's eyes to see the angel who carried a massive sword and told Balaam that but for the donkey moving out of his way, he would have surely killed Balaam on his journey. He did this as an illustration of the reckless path Balaam was on (going to serve a man that wanted to curse the people of God after God told him not to go). The angel reiterated the clear instruction of God to only say what God told him to say.

Upon arrival, Balaam told Balak to build seven

altars and to sacrifice on them. He did. Then Balaam blessed the people of Israel, as God instructed. Balak took Balaam to a different area, hoping for a different result. Again, Balaam blessed Israel. Finally, Balak took Balaam to the wasteland, here Balaam saw Israel lined up - tribe after tribe. The Spirit of God came over Balaam and God spoke through him. Not only did he bless Israel a third time, but he also cursed Balak and the neighboring nations, explaining to each how Israel was going to defeat them. In all, he gave seven prophecies (hence the seven altars he had Balak to build).

Balaam was a servant elected by God to share his message with specific audiences at specific times. But because Balaam was so blessed (he is one of a handful of men in the Bible that God actually came to speak with) his reputation placed him in the presence of kings on a regular basis. But with such a blessing comes great responsibility, if we are not careful, we can be mesmerized by the opportunities to enjoy riches and fame by lending those whose intentions God does not support our voice, time, resources, and attention. God created us as his workmanship to do good works, we are not to serve man, we were created to serve God.

When we are asked, where is our God? We know that we know what we know and can respond in great confidence. We will say of the Lord, "No misfortune is seen in Jacob, no misery observed in Israel. The Lord their God is with them; God brought them out of Egypt; they have the strength of a wild ox. There is no divination against Jacob, no evil omens against Israel. It will now be said of Jacob and of Israel, 'See what God has done!' The people rise like a lioness; they rouse themselves like a lion that does not rest till it devours its prey and drinks the blood of its victims." (50)

Prayer

Most Gracious and Heavenly Father,

God brought us out of Egypt; we have the strength of a wild ox. We devour hostile nations and break their bones in pieces; with our arrows we pierce them. Like a lion we crouch and lie down, like a lioness—who dares to rouse us? May those who bless us be blessed and those who curse us be cursed![51]

In Jesus' Name,
Amen

Turn to God

But now be strong, Zerubbabel,' declares the Lord. 'Be strong, Joshua son of Jozadak, the high priest. Be strong, all you people of the land,' declares the Lord, 'and work. For I am with you,' declares the Lord Almighty. This is what I covenanted with you when you came out of Egypt. And my Spirit remains among you. Do not fear.'

Haggai 2:4-5

There are moments when we get caught up in the whirlwind of life, the good times, the abundance and the fame of glory. But God wants our full attention and when we pay more attention to what is going on in our personal lives: family, business, or relationships, God will help us to focus on him.

When the people of Israel forgot God and did not honor him with their lives, building their own houses up, God stripped their abundance from them. Only when the prophet of the Lord, Haggai came to explain what had transpired did they repent and turn toward a life of obedience to God.

As they began to rebuild the temple of God, God began to restore their lives and livelihoods. In fact, God promised them that from that day forward he would bless them.

Our lives reflect the choices we have made. God desires to be first in our lives before any person, any job, any opportunity, or relationship. God is our everything and he desires to be treated as such. It is our responsibility to ensure that God and his sovereign will are at the center.

When we are asked, where is our God? We know that we know what we know and can respond in great confidence. We will say of the Lord, "He is with us." [(52)]

Prayer

Most Gracious and Heavenly Father,

You will shake the heavens and the earth. You will overturn royal thrones and shatter the power of the foreign kingdoms. You will overthrow chariots and their drivers; horses and their riders will fall, each by the sword of his brother. "'On that day,' declares the Lord Almighty, 'I will take you, my servant and I will make you like my signet ring, for I have chosen you,' declares the Lord Almighty. [(53)]

In Jesus' Name,
Amen

I Will Yet Praise Him

My tears have been my food day and night, while people say to me all day long, "Where is your God?"

Psalm 42:3

Hope deferred makes the heart sick. This is the reality for those of us who have been holding our breath, waiting for God to deliver us from what may feel like a nightmare that refuses to end.

In our hearts, we give God praise. In our secret place, we pray for protection and direction. In our minds and from our mouths, we tell our stories of obedience, patience, and the times we stumbled and fell.

But God. We wait on God because we trust Him. We sing his praise and pray without ceasing because he will not lie. Though our enemies surround us and point fingers to justify their poor actions and inaction, we stand still waiting on God to deliver us. We wait for God to instruct us on which way to go.

Despite our circumstance, or the taunts of our

enemies, we must hold on to our hope. We must cling to our beliefs, that God is for us and if God could be for us, who can be against us.

He is our rock, our shield, and our exceeding great reward. We are blessed and highly favored. God will deliver us from the hand of our enemy, he will deliver us from the oppressor. The enemies we see today, we will see no more.

When we are asked, where is our God? We know that we know what we know and can respond in great confidence. We will say of the Lord, "Our hope is in God, we will yet praise him, our Savior and our God." (53b)

Prayer

Most Gracious and Heavenly Father,

Vindicate us, our God, and plead our cause against an unfaithful nation. Rescue us from those who are deceitful and wicked. You are God our stronghold. Why have you rejected us? Why must we go about mourning, oppressed by our enemy? Send us your light and your faithful care, let them lead us; let them bring us to your holy mountain, to the place where you dwell. Then we will go to the altar of God, to God, our joy and our delight. We will praise you with the lyre, O God, our God. Why, our souls, are we downcast? Why so disturbed within us? We put our hope in God, for we will yet praise him, our Savior and our God. (54)

In Jesus' Name,
Amen

The Lord Lives!

He gives his king great victories; he shows unfailing love to his anointed, to David and to his descendants forever.

Psalm 18:50

God is waiting on us to open our mouths and ask him for what we need and desire. We are his good servants desiring to do his will, but we hesitate when it comes to calling on him. But God expects us to ask for help, especially when we need it most.

In Psalm 18, David is giving God glory and praise because he answered his prayer and helped him to have victory over his enemies. He begins simply by saying what we all feel, "I love you, Lord, my strength."[(55)]

But then David goes on to describe his dilemma of having so many enemies against him. David describes it as cords entangled around his neck, but he follows his description with God's reaction, which is one of anger. David felt that God was angry on his behalf because of how he'd been treated for so long.

You see, David was a good and honorable servant to God and man. He was humble and hard-working with a good attitude. He did not complain. Instead he showed up and did his best. David recognized that while he could not name many witnesses, he knew that God was aware and could see his due diligence, hard work, and accountability to God.

Not only was David a warrior, he also wrote praises to God on a regular basis. He communed with God and recognized God's sovereignty and love.

Like David, we must open our mouths to ask God for what we need and desire, but we must also praise and thank him for all he is, was, and will be. We can talk to God because he lives!

When we are asked, where is our God? We know that we know what we know and can respond in great confidence. We will say of the Lord, "I love you Lord, my strength."[(55)]

Prayer

Most Gracious and Heavenly Father,

You reached down from on high and took hold of us; you drew us out of deep waters. You rescued us from our powerful enemy, from our foes, who were too strong for us. They confronted us in the day of our disaster, but the Lord was our support. You brought us out into a spacious place; you rescued us because you delighted in us. The Lord has dealt with us according to our righteousness; according to the cleanness of our hands he has rewarded us. For we have kept the ways of the Lord; we are not guilty of turning from our God. All your laws are before us; we have not turned away from your decrees. We have been blameless before you and have kept ourselves from sin. The Lord has rewarded us according to our righteousness, according to the cleanness of our hands in his sight. [(56)]

In Jesus' Name,
Amen

Fortified Cities Cannot Stand Against God

Israel, however, put him to the sword and took over his land from the Arnon to the Jabbok, but only as far as the Ammonites, because their border was fortified.

Numbers 21:24

When Moses led the Israelites across the Red Sea and into their promised land, they had to cross many territories. In some areas, they were attacked, in others, they sought safe passage. When attacked, the Israelites prayed to God to help them defeat their enemies. In response, God gave their enemies into their hands. This happened as they journeyed through the Canaanite territory later named Hormah.

Then the Israelites simply asked to pass safely along the King's Highway through the land of the Amorites, but Sihon refused and marched his army out to fight them. Israel defeated them as well and took all the land of the Amorites, including Heshbon but stopped when they reached Ammonite territory because it was fortified. A fortified city is ready for attack as it is surrounded by well-built walls, defensive weapons, and soldiers ready for war. The Israelites were former slaves on a long journey to freedom, they were not prepared for war, they only had the will, favor, and angels of God to guide and protect them. So, the Israelites settled in the land of the Amorites and drove out all in the neighboring land of Jazer.

Then, when the king of Bashan came out to fight against them, they defeated their army as well and took their land captive. But they were unable to fight the Ammonites in the fortified city.

Years later, the king of the Ammonites decided he wanted the land where the Israelites were camped in Hormah. The leaders among the Gileadites knew a man, a mighty warrior and son of a prostitute, who they believed could help them win the battle against the Ammonites. But they'd publicly shamed the man and told him he had no right to their inheritance, driving him from their community. So when they came to him for help, he didn't trust them. But the community was desperate, and they promised him before God that they would make him a leader in their community - and they did just as they said.

The warrior, Jephthah, wrote a letter to the king of the Ammonites. He asked the king what right he had to come and try to take possession of their land; a land their God, the God of Israel had given to them?

But the king responded that the Israelites had stolen the land and had no rights to it. Jephthah answered that it was never the intent of the Israelites to occupy the land, only to pass through it. But when the people of the land refused to give them safe passage and attacked some of their people, they had no choice but to take the land by force. He also reminded them of Balak of Moab who never once attacked them and asked if the king thought he and his kingdom were better than Balak and his kingdom. Finally he shared that they were peaceably living next door for more than 300 years and asked them why they would attack now. The Ammonite king wanted to fight a war, so the king ignored Jephthah. Jephthah spoke a final word.

"I have not wronged you, but you are doing me wrong by waging war against me. Let the Lord, the Judge, decide the dispute this day between the Israelites and the Ammonites." (57)

Jephthah, the mighty warrior and ostracized son of a prostitute, made a sacred vow to the Lord. Then the Spirit of the Lord came over Jephthah that he devastated more than twenty towns and defeated the Ammonites, the fortified city that waged war on Israel.

The Israelites were simply trying to leave an oppressive state and settle into a promised land of peace and prosperity, but at every turn they were met by king after king who wanted to fight them and challenge the God they served.

When we are asked, where is our God? We know that we know what we know and can respond in great confidence. We will say of the Lord, "And from the time John the Baptist began preaching until now, the Kingdom of Heaven has been forcefully advancing, and violent people are attacking it." (58)

Prayer

Most Gracious and Heavenly Father,

We do not wrestle against flesh and blood, but against principalities, against powers, against the rulers of the darkness of this age, against spiritual hosts of wickedness in the heavenly places. [(59)] *My God, whom we praise, do not remain silent, for people who are wicked and deceitful have opened their mouths against us; they have spoken against us with lying tongues. With words of hatred they surround us; they attack us without cause. In return for our friendship they accuse us, but we are a people of prayer. They repay us evil for good, and hatred for our friendship. Appoint someone evil to oppose our enemy; let an accuser stand at his right hand. When he is tried, let him be found guilty, and may his prayers condemn him. May his days be few; may another take his place of leadership. May his children be fatherless and his wife a widow. May his children be wandering beggars; may they be driven from their ruined homes. May a creditor seize all he has; may strangers plunder the fruits of his labor. May no one extend kindness to him or take pity on his fatherless children. May his descendants be cut off, their names blotted out from the next generation. May the iniquity of his fathers be remembered before the Lord; may the sin of his mother never be blotted out. May their sins always remain before the Lord, that he may blot out their name from the earth. For he never thought of doing a kindness, but hounded to death the poor and the needy and the brokenhearted. He loved to pronounce a curse—may it come back on him. He found no pleasure in blessing—may it be far from him. He wore cursing as his garment; it entered into his body like water, into his bones like oil. May it be like a cloak wrapped about him, like a belt tied forever around him. May this be the Lord's payment to our accusers, to those who speak evil of us. But you, Sovereign Lord, help us for your name's sake; out of the goodness of your love, deliver us. For we are poor and needy, and our hearts are wounded within us. We fade away like an evening shadow; we are shaken off like a locust. Our knees give way from fasting; our body is thin and gaunt. We are an object of scorn to our accusers; when they see us, they shake their heads. Help us, Lord our God; save us according to your unfailing love. Let them know that it is your hand, that you, Lord, have done it. While they curse, may you bless; may those who attack us be put to shame, but may your servants rejoice. May our accusers be clothed with disgrace and wrapped in shame as in a cloak. With our mouths we will greatly extol the Lord; in the great throng of worshipers we will praise him. For he stands at the right hand of the needy, to save their lives from those who would condemn them.* [60]

In Jesus' Name,
Amen

Love God & Man

He answered, "'Love the Lord your God with all your heart and with all your soul and with all your strength and with all your mind'; and, 'Love your neighbor as yourself.'"

Luke 10:27

Who we are and how we show up in the world reflects what we believe. If we live our lives with only ourselves at the center, how can we possibly be considering God or others? If every decision we make is focused solely on our personal future and not how others are impacted by our decisions, how can we call ourselves children of God?

God gives each of us an opportunity to choose. We can choose each day to honor the Lord by giving him an opportunity to reach, teach, and breach our barriers. If we are daring enough to let God in, our lives will not only become an adventure, but Jesus will develop core beliefs within us that are unshakable... like loving others.

Loving others is a choice we must make too, and God doesn't make it easy by having us only love others that are important to us. God wants us to show his love to the most "unloving" people that he may penetrate their shells to allow light and love in.

Jesus drives it home for us when he shares the story of the Good Samaritan, a man without a responsibility risks his own life and makes a sacrifice to care for a man badly injured on a dangerous roadway, prone to crime. Consider your most dangerous neighborhood. Now picture the type of person you may avoid when you stop at a gas station, grocery store, or movie theater. Would you be willing to stop all that you are doing, endanger your own life to help that person, and pay for a safe place for them to heal? If so, you are the good neighbor God is trying to get all of us to become. No matter where we are on that journey, it begins with keeping God first in our lives.

If we are not connected to the vine (or in tune with God at all times), we will miss opportunities to show love to someone who really needs it. We have all experienced vulnerability in foreign places. It is not fun and we are often afraid to ask for help. When we intentionally walk with God, he keeps us more acutely aware of our surroundings and the care or concern of others. We can more easily recognize when people need help and understand ways we can assist them.

When we are asked, where is our God? We know that we know what we know and can respond in great confidence. We will say of the Lord, "I have been crucified with Christ and I no longer live, but Christ lives in me. The life I now live in the body, I live by faith in the Son of God, who loved me and gave himself for me." **(61)**

Prayer

Most Gracious and Heavenly Father,

You said, "Let light shine out of darkness," and made your light shine in our hearts to give us the light of the knowledge of God's glory displayed in the face of Christ. But we have this treasure in jars of clay to show that this all-surpassing power is from God and not from us. We are hard pressed on every side, but not crushed; perplexed, but not in despair; persecuted, but not abandoned; struck down, but not destroyed. We always carry around in our body the death of Jesus, so that the life of Jesus may also be revealed in our body. For we who are alive are always being given over to death for Jesus' sake, so that his life may also be revealed in our mortal body. So then, death is at work in us, but life is at work in you. It is written: "I believed; therefore I have spoken." Since we have that same spirit of faith, we also believe and therefore speak, because we know that the one who raised the Lord Jesus from the dead will also raise us with Jesus and present us with you to himself. All this is for the benefit of the kingdom, so that the grace that is reaching more and more people may cause thanksgiving to overflow to the glory of God. [62]

In Jesus' Name,
Amen

Faith Beyond Measure

Now faith is confidence in what we hope for and assurance about what we do not see. This is what the ancients were commended for.

Hebrews 11:1-2

What we do and believe in in faith may not be for us to see during our lifetime but will contribute to a foundation those who follow may stand upon.

The leaders of the civil rights movement boycotted, protested, and participated in sit-ins at lunch counters for the benefit of those who would follow. The right to vote, or purchase a home in the neighborhood we desire, or go to eat wherever we choose were not always options that were afforded to black people. To see a black person on the movie screen, serving as a doctor in the emergency room, or as a sitting judge on the Supreme Court were only dreams until someone accomplished it. Martin Luther King, Jr. died with a dream in his heart that he was never able to witness.

Our faith, hopes, and dreams may not be realized

in our lifetime. When I first realized this, it saddened me. But when I consider those who walked in faith before me, with hopes and dreams for a brighter future that they never realized, I recognized that I was in good company. David wanted to build a house for God but couldn't because he was a warrior. His son, Solomon built it instead. John Osteen worked diligently for God, building a large church and began a television ministry in Houston, Texas, but it was his son, Joel Osteen that realized his hopes of reaching millions of people with the word of God.

It is our dreams that give us the passion to live each day to the fullest. It is our faith fueled by what we believe will change the world or the part of the world God has elected we shine a light on. We may not get to see our dreams come to pass, but we can build a good foundation for them to stand upon.

Our faith will always be tested, twisted, tied up and turned upside down along the journey. We will be discouraged and disconnected from reality as we try to change the systems that need to be uprooted. We will question, doubt, and fear all at the same time, while pushing ourselves daily to take the next step of faith. We will need to lean and depend on the Word of God to teach us, the Holy Spirit to guide us, Jesus interceding for us, and the angels of heaven protecting us every step of the way.

When we are asked, where is our God? We know that we know what we know and can respond in great confidence. We will say of the Lord, "He is the resurrection and the life. The one who believes in him will live, even though they die." [63]

Prayer

Most Gracious and Heavenly Father,

We have faith and do not doubt. All things we ask in prayer, believing, we will receive. [(64)]

In Jesus' Name,
Amen

God Is

I will exalt you, my God the King; I will praise your name for ever and ever.

Psalm 145:1

God is magnificent. We are blessed because he does not see us as we are, he sees us as we were created to be. He sees our end and he develops us in his darkroom, preparing us for the destiny he defined long ago.

God takes the time to carefully nurture us and protect us. He also creates situations that will toughen us for resilience.

When the Israelites left slavery in Egypt, they were headed to the promised land of Canaan. Rather than take them the short route, which only took eleven days, he took them the long way around which took forty years. He did this because they were not ready to fight the kind of battles they would endure in Canaan. They also were unable to see themselves fully.

There is no battle we can fight and win without first identifying who we are in that fight. We must know ourselves fully before we can defend our beliefs or behaviors. We must know who God is and that he is our source, our beginning and our end; the reason we exist. The Israelites entered a season in which God (not their slave master) provided for their every need - water, shelter, food, protection, and guidance. We cannot know who we are without recognizing who God is.

When we are asked, where is our God? We know that we know what we know and can respond in great confidence. We will say of the Lord, "The Lord is trustworthy in all he promises and faithful in all he does." [65]

Prayer

Most Gracious and Heavenly Father,

Lord, you are righteous in all your ways and faithful in all you do. You are near to all who call on you, to all who call on you in truth. You fulfill the desires of those who fear you; you hear our cry and save us. You watch over all who love you, but all the wicked you will destroy. My mouth will speak in praise of you, Lord. Let every creature praise your holy name for ever and ever. [66]

In Jesus Name,
Amen

In the Solution

"Go and live in the village of Zarephath, near the city of Sidon. I have instructed a widow there to feed you."

I Kings 17:9

When we live for God, doing as he instructs, we may face adversity. We may see seasons of disruption, discord, and disengagement, but God will always care for us. We must trust God and do as he instructs because in our obedience, God becomes our solution.

In Israel, after King Ahab took office, he married a woman named Jezebel from Sidon (one of the wealthiest cities in the land) and adopted their religious customs, even building altars of worship and erecting false idols. God gave the prophet Elijah a prophetic message, decreeing a drought over the land. Then God told Elijah where to go to survive the drought.

Elijah went to live near a brook, where he drank water and the ravens brought him food each day. Eventually, due to the drought, the brook ran dry and God told Elijah where to go again.

As Elijah entered the town where God told him to go, he saw a widow with wood. He asked her for something to drink, then asked her to bring him some bread as well. The woman looked at him and explained her plight; she was down to her last. But Elijah insisted she care for him and he promised that God would supply her needs; she need not worry. She did as he asked, and God increased her little to much, providing all that she, her son and the prophet needed to survive.

But one day her son became ill and passed away. She was afraid it was a punishment for being a sinner, but Elijah prayed for her son and God brought him back to life. At this, the woman was thoroughly convinced that Elijah was indeed a prophet of God.

While we do not know what tomorrow may bring, we do know who holds tomorrow. When we are asked, where is our God? We know that we know what we know and can respond in great confidence. We will say of the Lord, "I cried out to him with my mouth; his praise was on my tongue. If I had cherished sin in my heart, the Lord would not have listened; but God has surely listened and has heard my prayer. Praise be to God, who has not rejected my prayer or withheld his love from me!" (67)

Prayer

Most Gracious and Heavenly Father,

When troubles of any kind come our way, we consider it an opportunity for great joy. We know that when our faith is tested, our endurance has a chance to grow. Let it grow, for when our endurance is fully developed, we will be perfect and complete, needing nothing. But we don't just listen to God's word. We must do what it says. Otherwise, we are only fooling ourselves. For if we listen to the word and don't obey, it is like glancing at our face in a mirror. We see ourself, walk away, and forget what we look like. But if we look carefully into the perfect law that sets us free, and if we do what it says and don't forget what we heard, then God will bless us for doing it. [(68)]

In Jesus' Name,
Amen

God is With Us

Then panic struck the whole army—those in the camp and field, and those in the outposts and raiding parties—and the ground shook. It was a panic sent by God.

I Samuel 14:15

The difficulty most of us have is seeing ourselves. We can see others and consider what they are doing incorrectly but it is difficult to see ourselves. Whether we are up or down, God is with us. He knows everything about us, and he has a poignant way of reminding us that his will must remain first in our lives.

The Israelites were at war against the Philistines. Saul's army was stationed near the Philistine camp, and he called for his entire army to fast. But Jonathon, Saul's son, and his armor bearer believed victory was available and decided to embark on the Philistine camp. Jonathan said to his armor bearer,

"Come, let's go over to the outpost of those uncircumcised men. Perhaps the Lord will act in our behalf. Nothing can hinder the Lord from saving, whether by many or by few."[69]

When the Philistine's saw the two men reveal themselves, they taunted them and dared them to meet them on the battlefield. Jonathan and his armor bearer fought back-to-back, Jonathan killing men in the front, his armor bearer killing men in the rear. They'd killed so many men that word got out in the camp and the other Philistines retreated in fear. Then the ground shook! God had caused a panic so great that Saul and the six hundred Israelite soldiers heard the commotion of them and decided to join in the battle. But before they went into battle, Saul asked for the priest to bring the ark of the covenant, as the commotion got louder, he asked the priest to withdraw his hand. Later when Saul and the army arrived, they saw that Jonathan, his armor bearer, Israelites, and Hebrews were at war with the Philistines.

God gave the Israelites the victory. The remaining Philistines ran away. As the Israelite men returned from battle, they stumbled upon a field filled with honey, but they were still fasting, so the soldiers did not dare taste it. But Jonathon and his armor bearer were unaware of the fast and ate, becoming immediately refreshed. The men told him of what his father decreed and why they were not eating. In an effort to dismiss his guilt, Jonathan brushed it off and told them had they eaten they would have fought a better fight. Then the men plundered the field of sheep and cattle, eating the meat raw.

When the priest witnessed this, he informed Saul who built his very first altar for God and called for his soldiers to return with their meat to eat it at their camp. The men did as instructed. Saul wanted to finish the job of defeating the Philistines, but the priest warned him to inquire of God first. God did not respond. Instead, he was silent. Saul realized that this was on account of sin and cast lots to see who was at fault. The lot fell to his son, Jonathan. Jonathan accepted his fate (a death sentence) but the soldiers stood up for him and would not allow him to be killed.

Even when we do not realize our faults, God is standing in the gap, there with us. When we have the audacity to trust God in the worst of circumstances, God is with us, and he will fight for us. We must seek God in all matters. Just as he fights for us in every battle, we must learn to give him the honor he deserves for he is good and his mercy endures forever. God deserves our honor and praise.

When we are asked, where is our God? We know that we know what we know and can respond in great confidence. We will say of the Lord, "All authority in heaven and on earth has been given to Jesus. Therefore we will go and make disciples of all nations, baptizing them in the name of the Father and of the Son and of the Holy Spirit, and teaching them to obey everything the Lord has commanded us. And surely he is with us always, to the very end of the age." [(70)]

Prayer

Most Gracious and Heavenly Father,

May God be gracious to us and bless us and make his face shine on us—so that your ways may be known on earth, your salvation among all nations. May the people praise you, God; may all the people praise you. May the nations be glad and sing for joy, for you rule the people with equity and guide the nations of the earth. May the people praise you, God; may all the people praise you. The land yields its harvest; God, our God, blesses us. May God bless us still, so that all the ends of the earth will fear him.[(71)]

In Jesus' Name,
Amen

Always & Forever

He raised Christ from the dead and seated him at his right hand in the heavenly realms, far above all rule and authority, power and dominion, and every name that is invoked, not only in the present age but also in the one to come. And God placed all things under his feet and appointed him to be head over everything for the church, which is his body, the fullness of him who fills everything in every way.

Ephesians 1:20b -23

Have you ever gone to an event and received VIP status? That status possibly allowed you to enter restricted areas, meet people that others would not have the opportunity to meet, and enjoy benefits such as swag, treats, meals, deluxe seating, etc. Well, as believers, we have unlimited access to every blessing fulfilled in Christ. Our belief and acceptance of his perfect gift of salvation allows us to speak the Word of God with authority, receive the covering of Jesus as he prays without ceasing, access to the unconditional mercy of God that is renewed each morning, and we even have sufficient provision and protection to supply our every need.

We have a Holy Spirit that prays for us, guides us when we need direction, and comforts us when we are down. We were also adopted as the children of God and granted to live an eternal life with Christ Jesus. Jesus promises he has prepared a place for us and will return to take us where he resides for when we are absent from the body, we are present with the Lord.

Most of all, we are the ambassadors of Christ, sharing his love on earth. His praise in our mouths, we honor him with our activity, we meditate on his word day and night, and we share his life with others so that they may know him. We love the Lord our God with all of our hearts, minds, and souls. We trust him to defend us, provide for us, teach us, and love us.

We are the hands and feet of God in the earth, experiencing his love and all of his benefits. The Lord was, is and shall always and forever be. When we are asked, where is our God? We know that we know what we know and can respond in great confidence. We will say of the Lord, "For to us a child is born, to us a son is given; and the government shall be upon his shoulder, and his name shall be called Wonderful Counselor, Mighty God, Everlasting Father, Prince of Peace." (72)

Prayer

Most Gracious and Heavenly Father,

Praise the Lord, our souls; all of our inmost beings, praise his holy name. Praise the Lord, our souls, and forget not all his benefits—who forgives all of our sins and heals all of our diseases, who redeems our lives from the pit and crowns us with love and compassion, who satisfies our desires with good things so that our youth is renewed like the eagle's. The Lord works righteousness and justice for all the oppressed. He made known his ways to Moses, his deeds to the people of Israel: The Lord is compassionate and gracious, slow to anger, abounding in love. He will not always accuse, nor will he harbor his anger forever; he does not treat us as our sins deserve or repay us according to our iniquities. For as high as the heavens are above the earth, so great is his love for those who fear him; as far as the east is from the west, so far has he removed our transgressions from us. As a father has compassion on his children, so the Lord has compassion on those who fear him; for he knows how we are formed, he remembers that we are dust. The life of mortals is like grass, they flourish like a flower of the field; the wind blows over it and it is gone, and its place remembers it no more. But from everlasting to everlasting the Lord's love is with those who fear him, and his righteousness with their children's children—with those who keep his covenant and remember to obey his precepts. The Lord has established his throne in heaven, and his kingdom rules over all. Praise the Lord, his angels, mighty ones who do his bidding, who obey his word. Praise the Lord, all his heavenly hosts, his servants who do his will. Praise the Lord, all his works everywhere in his dominion. Praise the Lord, our souls. [(73)]

In Jesus' Name,
Amen

Citations

1. Psalm 23
2. Psalm 91:2
3. Psalm 91:9-16
4. I Samuel 17:45 - 47
5. Psalm 143: 9-12
6. Psalm 66:5-7
7. Psalm 66:8-20
8. John1:1-5
9. Hebrews 11:3-6
10. Nehemiah 4:14
11. Psalm 16
12. Psalm 143:11-12
13. Isaiah 54:17
14. Psalm 109
15. Exodus 23:20-23
16. I Samuel 24:12-15
17. Romans 12:19
18. Ephesians 6:10-18
19. I Kings 18:36b-37
20. Psalm 29
21. Psalm 37:1-9
22. Psalm 63
23. Isaiah 43:16-21
24. Isaiah 43:1-13
25.Joel 2:25 -27
26. Psalm 119: 57-64
27. Job 39: 10-11; Psalm 149:4-9
28. Psalm 35:4-10
29. Judges 5:8-10
30. Judges 5:31
31. Psalm 40:4-13
32. Psalm 23:4

33. Deuteronomy 6:20-25
34. Isaiah 54:17
35. Psalm 91:9-16
36. Genesis 5:29
37. Genesis 6:6
38. Genesis 8:22
39. Psalm 104:1-9
40. Psalm 5:11
41. Psalm 6:8-10
42. I Samuel 16:18
43. Ephesians 2:10
44. Psalm 31:19-24
45. I Chronicles 16:8-14
46. Psalm 118:22-24
47. Esther 4:14
48. I Chronicles 16:28-29
49. I Chronicles 16:30-36
50. Numbers 23:21-24
51. Numbers 24:8-9
52. Haggai 1:13b
53. Haggai 2:21b-23
53b. Psalm 42:11b
54. Psalm 43
55. Psalm 18:1
56. Psalm 18:16-24
57. Judges 11:27
58. Matthew 11:12
59. Ephesians 6:12
60. Psalm 109
61. Galatians 2:20
62. 2 Corinthians 4:6-15
63. John 11:12
64. Matthew 21:21-22

65. Psalm 145:13b
66. Psalm 145:17-21
67. Psalm 66:17-20
68. James 1:2-4, 22-25
69. I Samuel 14:6
70. Matthew 28:18-20
71. Psalm 67
72. Isaiah 9:6
73. Psalm 103

About the Author

At the age of 9, Stephanie was molested by a friend of my family. In high school, she held the hand of a friend as he died from a fatal gun shot wound... As an adult, she was the victim of a violent acquaintance rape. Subsequently, she struggled with personal demons. But when she sought the Lord and his Word, her life was forever changed.

Give God ALL the Glory!

He is and will always be the head of my life. He is my joy, my strength, my everything.
My constant prayer is to be a perfect conduit of his message and love.

Stephanie was born in Muskogee, Oklahoma. She graduated from Putnam City North High School in 1994. She was married for 16 years. She is the mother of 3 beautiful daughters, and has a grandson named Levi. She graduated with her Associates in Technology, a Bachelor of Arts in Communications, and a Master of Arts in Communication with an emphasis in Political Communication.

She holds several design and technology certifications and has won numerous awards in that area. Stephanie has worked in television, print and web media for more than 16 years.

She is the owner of Moore Marketing and Communications. Her company offers strategic marketing and communication plans, media purchases, public relations, writing services, print services, graphic design and web design. Stephanie has also served as a poltical consultant for Governor, Lt. Governor, State Representative, Mayoral and City Council candidates.

Stephanie has created and sponsored teen etiquette and leadership programs for young ladies and young men. The program for young ladies is called, She's a BOSSE (A Beautiful Oasis of Success, Style and Elegance) and the young man's program is called Grindaholix: Young Men on the Rise.

To date, Stephanie has authored 25 books, 16 of which are daily devotionals. To learn more, visit mooretoread.com.

ECHOES
by
stephanie
d.
moore

31-Day Devotional
HIS
favor
stephanie
d.
It's not about obtaining HIS favor...
It's about recognizing you already have it!

The Living Proof!
A 31-DAY DEVOTIONAL
ON THE POWER OF YOUR WORDS
by
stephanie
d.
moore

NOTHING IS BIGGER THAN OUR GOD!
OBEY
obedience breaks every yoke
by
stephanie
d.
moore
31 Day
Devotional
Divine Leadership

31-Day Devotional
INTO THE
Promised
Land
stephanie
d.
moore
Desperately Seeking the Presence of God
in the Wilderness on Your Journey
INTO THE PROMISED LAND!

BETRAYED
FAMILY SECRETS

by
stephanie
d.
moore

31 DAY
DEVOTIONAL
2 Corinthians 9:8
ABUNDANCE
Faith & Wisdom
MOVING YOUR MOUNTAIN
by
stephanie
d.
moore

blush
you are the apple of my eye
A 31-DAY DEVOTIONAL
OF GOD'S UNENDING LOVE FOR YOU
stephanie
d.
moore

I AM
DELIVERED!
by
stephanie
d.
moore
HIS GRACE
HIS STRENGTH

www.ingramcontent.com/pod-product-compliance
Lightning Source LLC
LaVergne TN
LVHW010931110826
845149LV00013B/2545

* 9 7 8 1 9 5 5 5 4 4 4 1 2 *